insight text guide

Leonie Keaney

Fly Away Peter

David Malouf

First published in 1998, reprinted in 2020, 2021, 2023

Insight Publications Pty Ltd
3/350 Charman Road
Cheltenham VIC 3192
Australia
Tel: +61 3 8571 4950
Fax: +61 3 8571 0257
Email: books@insightpublications.com.au

www.insightpublications.com.au

National Library of Australia Cataloguing-in-Publication entry:
Keaney, Leonie.
David Malouf's Fly Away Peter.
Bibliography.
For secondary school students.
ISBN 9781875882137 (pbk.)
1. Malouf, David, 1934-. Fly Away Peter.
2. Malouf, David, 1934-, Criticism and Interpretation.
I. Title.
A823.3

Other ISBNs:
9781922378774 (digital)
9781922378781 (bundle: print + digital)

Cover design by Gisela Beer

The editors and publishers wish to acknowledge the kind permission of Penguin Books Australia to reprint extracts from *Fly Away Peter* by David Malouf.

Printed in Australia by Ligare Book Printers

contents

CHARACTER MAP

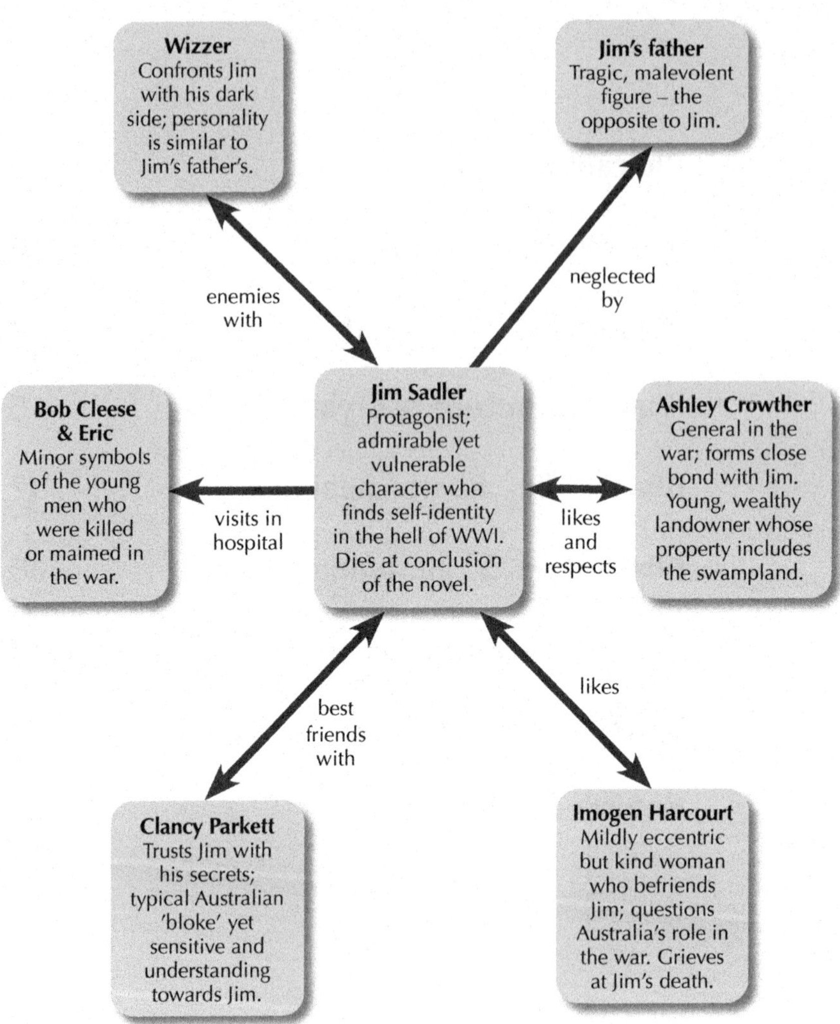

INTRODUCTION

David Malouf is one of Australia's most celebrated writers. Winner of the prestigious Dublin Prize for Literature in 1996 for his book *Remembering Babylon*, Malouf's fame is now international. Most of his work is concerned with Australia, its developing identity, and its sense of self. *Fly Away Peter*, one of his earlier works, published in 1982, is a fine example of this exploration.

The book is set in Australia and Europe during World War I and presents a harsh and confronting picture of the experience of that war for so many young Australian men. The absurdity of trench warfare is highlighted in detail in the months and years that were spent fighting water, mud, rats and dead bodies for no gain in territory and great loss of life. Australia's involvement in the first place is seen as equally absurd, based as it is on colonial ties which demand loyalty to Britain against an enemy unknown to most of the soldiers. It was in this war, however, that the Anzac legend was born, a founding element in the Australian national psyche. Malouf is not seeking to explain our participation in the war so much as to explore the meaning of the legend then and now.

The novel is about much more than just the war, however. Malouf uses it to examine the individual's place in a complex, multi-layered world and the meaning this has in people's lives, especially in relation to Australian culture. He is also concerned with the notion of land, connections with it and the meaning this has in people's lives – especially in Australia. In the characters of Jim and Ashley, bonded as they are by their connection with the land, he hints at the significance of land for Australia's original inhabitants, a theme he explores more fully in *Remembering Babylon*. Class, its origins in the British class system and its adaptation for good or ill, is also explored, as are issues of friendship, violence and the transient nature of human life.

Above all, however, Malouf writes about the contrast and the links between good and bad, violence and tranquillity, innocence and experience, life and death – the light and the dark sides of the mind. In doing so he asserts that without acknowledgement and acceptance of both, an individual's self-knowledge is incomplete, and human life unfulfilled.

BACKGROUND & CONTEXT

World War I

Australia became involved in World War I because of its colonial ties with Britain. In 1914 Australia was only thirteen years into nationhood. Ninety-eight per cent of all those living in Australia were of Anglo-Celtic origin. The view most Australians had of themselves was that they were British subjects in a new land and their loyalty was as much to Britain and its empire as to any sense of Australian identity. In its social life, cultural practices and ethnic values Australia was an outpost of British life. The public admiration for all things British contributed to the inferiority complex and the cultural cringe that some believe Australia is yet to throw off.

It is in this Australia that we meet Jim Saddler and his friends Ashley Crowther and Imogen Harcourt. It is in this Australia that we see the enthusiastic, almost delirious response to the outbreak of World War I, depicted in Chapter 5, and the decisions of many of the young men of that generation to go and be a part of the great adventure which the war was meant to be.

World War I was essentially a colonial war. The grab for power and territory which in the latter part of the nineteenth century had seen most of Africa and a good deal of Asia taken over by the major European powers finally spilled over into a bitter conflict for supremacy in Europe itself. Distance and limited communications meant that the vast majority of Australians knew little and understood less of the circumstances that led to the declaration of war by Britain against Germany in September 1914. Yet the response was volcanic. The enemy 'Hun' was effectively and almost instantly demonised into a threat to all things good, and across the country young men began queuing up to enlist.

Dubbed at the time the 'war to end all wars' and 'The Great War', the 1914–18 war proved to be neither. However, it was a source of almost universal shock at just how horrifying and evil war could be. It was not long before the euphoria of the outbreak disappeared and was replaced by the misery of injury, loss and death. Despite its isolation and small population, Australia lost more men per head of population than any other country involved. Thus the Anzac legend has an enduring place in the national psyche and writers such as Malouf have explored this searing experience.

Class

Australian society inherited much from its British origins, among other things a form of its class system. The experience of living in a 'new land', the pioneer life with its attendant hardships and the economic growth that accompanied the rapid rise in population at the end of the nineteenth century all contributed to the emergence of the notion of Australia as an egalitarian society in which the binds of class, which so restricted individuals in the old world, no longer applied. While this was so to a degree, the adaptation and imitation of so much of British life meant that the trappings of class were never really expunged. We see a clear example of how class remained a determining factor in the opportunities and experiences life presented in the characters of Jim and Ashley.

Ashley has inherited his land from his father and grandfather. After education in England – an adequate education simply not possible for a young man in Australia at the time – he returns to take up his holding. Jim, his worker, is his social inferior, not in the way Ashley treats him but simply because of their social heritage – the way they dress, speak, the sort of cigarettes they smoke. Jim is not a serf, as in the feudal days without basic human rights, but the two men are as culturally different as if they came from different ends of the globe and not from the same sparsely populated part of southern Queensland. One of Malouf's triumphs is that he demonstrates that the bonds uniting these two young men transcend the class boundary between them.

GENRE, STRUCTURE & STYLE

Genre

Fly Away Peter is a powerful and poetic novel, simple yet profound. Because it is short it is more like a novella – a brief fictional prose narrative.

The novel develops its story around a single main character – Jim Saddler – who largely gives the work its concentrated focus. *Fly Away Peter* tells what is in one way a traditional story – that of one man's physical and spiritual journey from innocence to experience, in this case through Jim's move from Australia to Europe when he joins up to fight in World War I. As Jim Saddler is thrust into the horrors and destruction of the war he sees that his state of 'dangerous innocence' (p.107) failed to take into account the 'dark side' of himself and of life. At the point of death he recognises his uniqueness within his ordinariness and reconciles the brutalities and wasted lives of the war experience with the innocence and simplicity of ordinary life.

The depth of exploration of the many interrelated themes in the novel is achieved, in part, through Malouf's powerful imagery that develops motifs throughout the work. In this, brevity is used to great advantage as we can carry the subtly developed images forward in our own minds in a way not dissimilar to the process of understanding – some would say enlightenment – that Jim Saddler experiences. The use of contrasts underpins the book – it is manifest in the characters, in the central idea of binary opposites – for example, beauty and horror, ordinariness and uniqueness within the one creature or human being, in the two countries, and in the key images. The overarching imagery, drawn from birds and birdlife, is often delicate and beautiful, capturing human sensitivity – especially in Jim Saddler's reverence towards migratory birds – and the enduring instinct for survival in the face of war's destructive forces.

The story

Fly Away Peter is primarily about Jim Saddler's journey from innocence to experience. It celebrates an ordinary, self-effacing man's life, emphasising its richness and complexity. Jim is the focus of the whole work and the source of the ideas Malouf explores in this novel.

Jim Saddler's love and understanding of the birdlife along the Queensland coast where he lives brings him into contact with Ashley Crowther, the wealthy young landowner whose holding includes the swampland where Jim pursues his hobby. Separately, Jim meets Imogen Harcourt, a photographer, who through her pictures adds a new dimension to Jim's sense of the birds' lives. Her photo of the sandpiper is so perfect he realises that *'this is the moment when we see into the creature's unique life'* (p.28). Through Jim the three become partners in recording the birdlife of the swampland – the sanctuary.

The outbreak of war intrudes on their tranquil lives. Both Jim and Ashley find themselves on the battlefields of France. Jim is plunged into the flip side of the natural beauty he has left behind. The violence and despair of the war threatens to destroy him emotionally as well as physically. Confronted by the 'dark side of his head' (p.59), Jim faces up to his own fear and develops a new and deeper understanding of the meaning of his own life, and of all life. He dies, but is triumphant.

At home, Imogen is left to mourn, bewildered by the extent of her loss. In searching for some meaning in Jim's apparently senseless death she recognises the value and the passing nature of the individual's existence. She concludes that 'A life wasn't *for* anything, it simply was' (p.140).

Structure

The novel divides very clearly into two halves. This structure not only serves the story but reflects the primary theme of the writer – that of binary opposites.

Like a coin there are two sides to all experience, all life, all personalities. You can't have one without the other, although one may be more obvious and the other lies dormant. So, where there is good, there must be bad, where there is peace there must also be war, and so on with joy and despair, light and dark, knowledge and ignorance.

The first eight chapters are set in the paradise of the bird sanctuary on Ashley Crowther's land in southern Queensland. Here, birdlife is in balance with the environment. Each bird knows its place, its role. The birds confidently defy human odds by migrating year after year with the seasons, travelling thousands of miles to reach the place where they are meant to be. They amaze and entrance Jim. He also, though human, is in touch with the environment, understanding its needs and respectful of the need to preserve its balance. On this side of the coin all is good, tranquil and at peace. The partnership Jim, Ashley and Imogen form reflects this further. Though divided by class, gender and experience they are brought together and work in unison because of the birds, each contributing a different but significant element to the task of recording the birdlife of the sanctuary. The images in this part of the book all reflect peace, serenity and the pre-eminence of the natural order of things.

The second half, beginning with Chapter 9, takes Jim and the reader into the reverse of paradise. Trench warfare is brutal, dehumanising, life-sapping, evil. Here the balance of nature has been turned upside down. There is annihilation not regeneration. The young men dying each day in the mud will not return, as the birds do, to the other side of the world. Here the images are of destruction, disintegration and of a world out of order.

Despite the contrast, however, there are links between the two 'sides' Malouf presents. In the alien world Jim finds himself in when training on Salisbury Plain, he is reassured by 'the presence of the birds that allowed [him] to make a map in his head of how the parts of his life were connected' (p.62). There is the recurring image of the teeming masses: of the birds and of the soldiers on the battlefield. Each individual life is part of a vast, complex design. Within the flocks of birds there are individuals such as the sandpiper, who have a beginning and an end and a meaning. Within the flock of people, there is Jim.

In the end the story returns to Australia and Imogen alone and grief-stricken. There is completion and symmetry in this. The depth of Imogen's loss and her realisation and acceptance that Jim's life was not necessarily cut short – it simply *was* – sees both she and Jim triumphant and, like the birds, part of the continuing rich pattern of existence.

Style and language

Malouf's combination of realism – that is, the lifelike and credible depiction of the lives of the characters and the war experience – with the poetic is the source of much of this novel's power. The central concept of binary opposites penetrates this novel and demonstrates Malouf's command of language – not just in his creation of beauty and horror, gentleness and harshness, sensitivity and brutality and so on, but also in his vision of the fundamental role of opposites that need to be reconciled, somehow, in life.

The power of images

Images play a fundamental role in *Fly Away Peter*. They are crucial to the creation of Jim Saddler's character and his experiences. Images of birds and his response to birdlife are of particular significance. Through Malouf's careful descriptions of the dunlin, for example, we are led to see similarities between it and Jim. The small plain dunlin, a tiny bird that can make the huge journey to the other side of the earth annually with unerring accuracy, to some extent mirrors Jim's qualities and life. There are simple but significant parallels at work: the dunlin is ordinary, inconspicuous, of no great importance in the larger scheme of things, yet also unique, unaware of the danger of its migratory journey which it undertakes by instinct. In this, it is similar to Jim's rather sudden decision to go to war on the other side of the world; although he knows about the risk to life, he has no real sense of just what that will mean.

The war is described through graphic images of its horror: its smell 'of damp earthwalls and rotting planks, of mud impregnated with gas, of decaying corpses' (p.80) for example. At times we move into Jim's direct and awful experience – when for instance he thought Clancy had touched him on the back of the neck in the trench but 'it was the earth behind him, quietly moving. Suddenly it collapsed, and a whole corpse lurched out of the wall and hurled itself upon him' (p.83). This moves beyond mere description as the image haunts Jim, showing how close death is and forewarning that death's 'touch' is inevitable. The whole corpse lurching out of the wall and hurling itself upon Jim prefigures the unexpectedness and horror of Clancy Parkett's death. However, this early direct contact with death pales before the frightful reality of Clancy being blasted out existence. This is a particularised image of war, but generalised images abound and are worth close attention as they give an overall idea of the war – the bigger picture.

Images and themes

Through his simple and accessible language and the development of key images, David Malouf explores complex and interrelated themes. One theme that is central to the novel is the act of imagining. We perceive this process through the depiction of Jim Saddler's sensibilities. Jim on many occasions is shown bringing things into focus through concentrating his mind in order to experience the very essence of life. This is particularly clear in his response to Imogen Harcourt's photo of the sandpiper:

Key quote

> Perfect. Every speckle, every stripe on the side where it faded off into the white of the underbelly, the keen eye in the lifted head – he felt oddly moved to see the same bird in this other dimension. Moved too at the trouble it must have taken, and the quick choices, to get just that stance ... Did she know so much about birds? Or did some intuition guide her? *This is it; this is the moment when we see into the creature's unique life*. That too might be a gift. (p.28)

This imaginative act of Jim's (and of Malouf's writing) shows how deeply Jim desires to grasp the essence of life – thereby introducing that major theme: what is life? This is explored through Jim's life experiences that include the importance of photography and The Book, both methods of capturing and recording life. However, for these processes to be significant they have to be responded to, interpreted, grasped by the human mind and spirit. In the moment of recognising that Imogen has captured the essence of the sandpiper, Jim himself is so concentrated that he too is revealed in his essential being. Imogen Harcourt recognises this when, grieving for Jim's wasted life, she recalls this very image cited above:

Key quote

> Her pain lay in the acute vision she had had of his sitting as she had seen him on that first day, all his intense being concentrated on the picture she had taken of the sandpiper ... his mind, absorbed in the uniqueness of the small creature as the camera had caught it just at that moment ... and in entering that one moment of the bird's life ... bringing up to the moment, in her vision of him, his own being that was just so very like the birds, alert, unique, utterly present. (p.140)

Here memory plays a crucial role in her search for life's meaning. Jim intensely gazing at her photograph captures for her his essence. She sees, through that remembered image, that 'that is what life meant, a unique presence, and it was essential in every creature' (p.140). She accepts Jim's death by seeing that the question 'What is life *for*?' leads her away from understanding and coming to terms with death. What really matters is that life *is*. Its existence in all its complexity (the many levels and paradoxes of existence) and simplicity (Jim's life in Australia) and intensity (Jim focused on the photo) and randomness (war) and order (The Book and the photos) ultimately cannot be explained – it has to be accepted as it *is*. Malouf explores this question through images, their cumulative effect as they are revisited, events, and the direct thoughts of his characters.

Images and reconciling opposites

The novel confronts a difficult question – how do we make sense of the apparent randomness of life and death? How do we reconcile the intense vibrancy of not only the mystery and wonder of life itself but of its destruction and loss? Jim is shown to achieve this when he is wounded (pp.120–1) through a vision that gives him an aerial perspective of the war – an all-seeing distant viewpoint like that of a bird. This enables him to hold in his mind an 'immensely expanded' map that now can see men's war activities and the small domestic lives of nature's creatures, that can see the suffering and death and his own life 'neither more nor less important than the rest' (p.123) as part of a whole.

Malouf has carefully developed the images of maps and the power of aerial perspectives, both through birds and flying in Ashley's bi-plane. Through Jim's vision where 'perhaps he had, in some part of himself, taken on the nature of a bird; though it was with a human eye that he saw' (p.112), Malouf suggests that the power of the mind, the imagination and the human spirit are able to integrate experience in a meaningful and intuitive understanding of life. We witness, and imaginatively share, Jim reconciling the extremes of his life experience, recognising that he is both ordinary and unique, and accepting that life *is* – a kind of continuum that is incomplete without apparently irreconcilable opposites.

Images, through their power to work both literally and metaphorically through a range of associations, and to gather meaning – an important element of their power – are central to the imaginative creation of this novel's characters and the exploration of its deepest issues.

CHAPTER-BY-CHAPTER ANALYSIS

Chapter 1 (pp.1–8)

The opening chapter introduces all the main themes and ideas of the novel, and, by name or association, the characters.

Key scenes

Swampland, birds (pp.1–2); Jim's mental map and attitude to the birds (pp.2–3); Ashley Crowther introduced (pp.3–5); Jim's father (pp.5–6).

The story opens with Jim in the swampland watching birds and being distracted by a bi-plane doing circles in the sky nearby. He is unsettled by this intrusion of the human world into that of the birds. Jim has 'a map ... in his head' (p.2) of the whole area, this Garden of Eden, teeming with life and richness. Nature is in balance it seems, and the birds are in happy command of their territory. It is Jim who is the strange creature: an intruder, albeit a respectful one. He recognises all of them and knows the pattern of their lives. This one has come from Siberia, this from China. Many are from Europe, the other side of the world, which is soon to turn Jim's world upside down.

The bi-plane belongs to Ashley Crowther, the young and wealthy landowner. His property includes the swampland. He is entertaining guests, providing them with flights around the area – something Jim doesn't need because, like the hawk, he is able to 'see' it from on high. Ashley, like the birds, has recently returned from Europe. After education in England he has taken up his inheritance and is effectively the local squire. The distinction between his and Jim's lives is thus clearly drawn, yet we also learn that it is Ashley who has provided the field glasses for Jim. The two share an interest in the birds and Ashley has brought the idea to record the comings and goings of the swampland newly from Europe. The job has liberated Jim, 'made free of his own life', the 'flat' life which his father declares as inevitable 'for the likes of us' (p.5).

Jim feels a strong connection with Ashley despite the gulf of class difference that lies between them. The silence that can exist between them is bonding and companionable and Ashley recognises 'that Jim too had rights here, that these acres might also belong, though in another manner, to him' (p.7). The strong friendship between the two young men contrasts dramatically with Jim's relationship with his own father. The father's ferocious personality and savagery is a portent of the violence which Jim will encounter later and which he fears he will be 'infected' by.

Finally, though she doesn't appear herself, Imogen's photos are anticipated in the pictures of the birds Jim 'frames' in his field glasses. He has been watching a swamphen for nearly an hour so captivated is he by the intensity of its small life. No wonder he is so struck by Imogen's images when he first sees them.

The chapter ends with Jim dismissing his father's mean-spirited view of the world and embracing Ashley's generous one which made room for both him and the birds – 'even the most alien' (p.8). We are left with a very clear view of the protagonist, Jim Saddler. Our view of others will be through him and the perspective on events will be his.

Chapter 2 (pp.9–19)

This chapter is devoted to introducing Ashley, who is part of the class system that has been adopted in part from the British aristocracy. His friendship with Jim transcends class differences through their mutual interest in nature.

Key scenes

Ashley's English experiences (pp.9–10); attitude to his return to Australia (pp.10–11); Ashley's attitude to the landscape (p.11); his meeting with Jim (pp.15–18); he offers Jim work (pp.18–19).

While Australia by 1914 had long demonstrated that it accepted and encouraged all who wanted to make a go of it, and that titles carried little weight, the power of inherited wealth, especially through land, nonetheless continued to determine prosperity in the same way it did in England. As well, most of those who owned large amounts of land in Australia imitated the British upper class in the houses they built and the way they spoke and dressed and socialised.

Ashley is typical of his class. He has been to England to be educated as was expected of such young men. After Cambridge, however, he decided to return to Australia. Despite the derision of his companions who can't believe he would willingly live in such a barbaric place as outback Australia without the sophistication of European life, he is pleased to be back in what he regards as his home, 'what came closest to the centre of his being' (p.11). He is able to migrate, like the birds and unlike some of his peers. Thus his meeting with Jim and their easy collusion in the recording of the life of the sanctuary.

Despite Ashley's connection with his land and his comfort with being in Australia – 'It [the land] might be old, even very old, but it was more open than Europe to what was still to come' (p.15) – he nonetheless seeks to re-create European social life on his property with weekend parties, tennis, picnics and joy rides with Bert in his bi-plane. These activities, his clothes and his cigarettes all underscore the point that Ashley is unlike Jim in his origins, family, traditions and expectations.

The two young men are brought together by more powerful forces than those of class. In their interest in the birds they are equals. Jim, even, is superior, with his knowledge of the birdlife and their behaviour. Jim has what Ashley needs and thus he is employed to observe the birds. The levelling effect of their work together is mirrored later on in their experiences in the war when wealth and status do not matter when all are being slaughtered.

There is delightful irony at the end of this chapter when Ashley assures Jim when offering him the work, 'I'd make it worth your while' (p.19). Jim could want for nothing more than what Ashley has suggested to him. They shake on it and so are united – more than they can imagine.

Chapter 3 (pp.20–9)

Imogen Harcourt, an unusual and striking character, is the focus here.

Key scenes

Jim watching the sandpiper (pp.20–1); Jim sees Imogen taking photos (pp.21–2); Jim visits Imogen (pp.23–4); Jim sees the photo of the sandpiper (pp.27–9).

It is 1914. Imogen Harcourt is a woman in her fifties who lives alone, pursues photography – still in its infancy – and like many younger women 'spoke straight up at you' (p.26). She came to Australia originally with her brother, seeking a fortune, but when he returned to England, she decided to stay. Imogen is an independent woman, in control of her life. Jim finds that 'he understood almost everything she said straight off, and this was unusual' (p.27).

Jim is watching a sandpiper through his glasses. He is amazed by its presence in the sanctuary as it had been 'on the other side of the earth ... only weeks ago' (p.20). He wonders if, like Jim himself, the bird has a map in its head. Imogen appears suddenly in his view. She too has the sandpiper in her sights. The first we know of her is her physical appearance – grey skirt, grey curls under a bonnet, boots. It would be easy to jump to the conclusion that she is eccentric and easily dismissed but Jim observes quickly that she is 'independent but not odd' (p.26).

Jim follows Imogen to her house and introduces himself. Their meeting is an easy one with Imogen asking him to wait at first and then opening the conversation with 'Would you like tea?' (p.25). She shows him her photo of the sandpiper and immediately Jim recognises the new dimension that Imogen's pictures will bring to his knowledge of the birds: '*This is the moment when we see into the creature's unique life*' (p.28).

Very soon Jim connects Ashley with Imogen and 'So they became partners, all three, and a week later Jim told her of the sanctuary, actually using the word out loud for the first time' (p.28). This annunciation by him confirms that this place is paradise, speaking the word actually making it true.

Chapter 4 (pp.30–5)

Jim takes parties of Ashley's friends on boat trips around the swamplands to see the birds. In these expeditions the two parts of Ashley's life come together and he is able to express something essential to himself. The first reference to the imminent war in Europe occurs here (p.34).

On the one hand the boat trips are reminiscent of Ashley's days in England, punting on the Cam (the Cambridge River at the university). The company is young and wealthy, the conversation is chatty rather than meaningful and the birds are regarded as Ashley's collector's items – instead of 'Meissen figures or Oriental mats' (p.33) – the kind of thing a wealthy young man might collect in order to occupy his time. On the other hand, the trips have an almost spiritual quality for Ashley. He is very in touch with the great age of the land he is custodian of. He wonders if the birds are in fact 'extravagantly disguised spirits of another order of existence', suggesting the imagery of Aboriginal dreaming (p.31). He is shocked by the 'otherness of their being [and] could never quite accept that they were, he and these creatures, of the same world' (p.33).

The conduit for these two parts of Ashley's life is Jim. Not only is Jim the authority on the birds who gives the boat trips their novelty value and substance, it is his knowledge that awakens Ashley to the true meaning of observing the birdlife of the swamp. It is not for trophies or status at having found this or that, or to claim recognition of some rare creature. It is to know more of oneself and one's place in the world – the larger world of creation and all of life. In this world Ashley and Jim are central players as well as part of the crowd. The significance of their lives as individuals in the world is profound – but only as profound as that of other lives in the continuing evolving pattern.

The somewhat inane chatter of the boat party leads Jim to concede that 'Europe must be a mad place' (p.34) and it is in this chapter that for the first time the imminent war there is mentioned. In the light of what happens later, this episode has the quality of an idyll, a brief moment of tranquillity and beauty before the dreadful storm which is to come. The comfortable 'double silence' that exists between Ashley and Jim at the end of the chapter confirms the sense of balance between them and their world.

Chapter 5 (pp.36–43)

The war has finally come – the news arriving late to Brisbane and even later to Jim.

Key scenes

When confronted with the question of joining up Jim asks, '"Why?" ... in a last moment of innocence' (p.37); Jim visits hotels and imbibes the war euphoria (pp.38–9); Brisbane's crowded night-time streets make Jim nervous about the future (pp.42–3).

Jim is a little surprised at the great excitement in Brisbane and does not share immediately the sense of great adventure that the outbreak of war engendered in many young Australians at the time. He is very aware, however, that a strong, young man like himself would go – it was expected, even assumed. The 'cause' has been appropriated fully by the revellers in the city, all convinced of the rightness of their side despite knowing little of the origin or real purpose of the hostilities.

The noise and disturbance in Brisbane, and the ugly racist language of Jim's companion, contrast dramatically with the peace of the sanctuary he has so recently left. Already it seems the war is creating violence and chaos even before anyone has boarded a troop ship. Jim asks himself, *'Is this what it will be like from now on? ... Will I get used to it?'* (p.42). The answers are 'yes' and 'no' respectively. The reader knows this and must wonder if Jim is asking rhetorically.

But Jim is swept along by the tide of 'loose excitement that had been around all day' (p.42). He is a typical young man of his time in many ways and readily takes the opportunity offered to him by Connie when she asks him to go home with her to give him 'something to remember before he went' (p.39). He is pleased with himself at the end of the afternoon and enjoys the liveliness as he walks back through town. He cannot, however, reassure himself that nothing will change. Back home, when Imogen asks him about Brisbane and if anything is going on there, his reply of 'the war. Not much otherwise' (p.43) is full of irony.

Chapter 6 (pp.44–6)

This very brief chapter is devoted to the work of the recording of the birds and their activities which Jim, Ashley and Imogen have undertaken together.

Key scene

Jim's thoughts on recording the birds' lives (p.45).

Jim's careful recording in copybook writing gives greater significance to the presence of the birds and to the work of the three in documenting the life of the sanctuary. For Jim, his entries in The Book and Imogen's photos give the birds 'existence in another form, recognising their place in the landscape, or his stretch of it' (p.45). Ashley exclaims at the beauty of The Book 'as he never did for the actual birds, to which he only brought his silence' (p.46). In Jim's mind 'that was right' as it not only expresses Jim's reverence towards the birds but also the 'way Ashley's reaction mirrored his own' (p.46). The recording provides another 'sanctuary' for the birds, giving them 'a permanent place in the world' (p.45). The occasion of Ashley's marriage is marked with the presentation of the first Book and Imogen's first photos to accompany it.

Chapter 7 (pp.47–50)

This very short chapter is concerned with the arrival of the dunlin, a bird common in Imogen Harcourt's home in England but never before sighted by Jim. The bird represents the essence of Malouf's thoughts on binary opposites and is symbolic of Jim in many ways.

Key scenes

Jim sights the dunlin and Imogen's reactions (pp.48–9); photographing the dunlin (pp.49–50).

The dunlin is an everyday sight where Imogen comes from but is exotic and precious to Jim. It is in many ways a different creature to him, even sounding different in his pronunciation. Imogen laughs at 'the newness of the old word now that it had arrived on this side of the globe' (pp.48–9). There is great excitement that theirs must be a first sighting of the creature in this part of Australia. Jim is dizzy with success that 'we've discovered something!' (p.50). Imogen is less so because she regards the bird as so ordinary but 'she was moved ... to be included. She had come so far to where everything was reversed that even that didn't surprise her' (p.50). Here are many images of the two-sidedness of everything – new is old, exotic is ordinary, common is rare.

Like the dunlin, Jim – so ordinary, so typical of Australia and his times – will be rare and exotic when he finds himself on the other side of the world. He too will be like the 'refugee' bird, standing out in the alien world he finds himself in. He will still be Jim, as the bird remains itself, but there will be parts of himself he has not known that will reveal themselves and seem new – the way the bird's name sounded new.

Chapter 8 (pp.51–8)

This chapter focuses on Jim's changing viewpoints and attitudes to life.

Key scenes

Jim's attitude to the bi-plane (pp.51–2); the flight gives Jim a mental aerial map (p.55); Jim's decision to go to the war (p.56); his father's approval in a fleeting show of affection for Jim (p.58).

Despite his reluctance, Jim agrees to take a ride in Ashley's bi-plane. He is uneasy with the idea of humans flying as it challenges his view of the rightness of things. Earth is for humans, the sky belongs to the birds. He approaches the flight with some sense of dread and of his own 'heaviness'. The 'monstrous cage' (p.52) seems to be a bastardised version of the magnificence of bird flight and Jim is also already aware that these machines have now become weapons of destruction in the war.

Nonetheless, once up in the sky Jim is filled with wonder – not because he is flying but because he can appreciate for the first time the map the birds carry in their heads and realises that it is not very different from his own: 'the map in his own head, which he had tested and found accurate, might be related to the one the birds carried in theirs, which allowed them to find their way' (p.55).

The war has developed significantly with the losses at Gallipoli already having an impact on Australians and how they see themselves. The euphoria has gone, but it is in this new atmosphere that Jim decides to go. It is also notable that it is while he is flying that he makes the decision or comes to the realisation that he will go to the war. He seems weighed down, not by a sense that he will die, but by an awareness that this is the end of his life as he has known it – things will never be the same. From the plane he has 'his last vision of the world he knew' (p.55). His decision has drawn a line 'between the past and what was to come, the two parts of his life' (p.58). His single rationale for going is that 'he would never understand, when it was over, why his life and everything he had known were so changed' (p.57).

Jim tells Ashley who accepts his decision without question. In their typical unspoken communication, each acknowledges that the job will be there for Jim when he returns because 'the timespan for [the birds] was more or less infinite' (p.57). Importantly, Ashley will also go, but in a few months and as an officer, a position reflecting his wealth, status and class. Imogen is angry that Jim is going, her commonsense personality rejecting what she sees as the nonsense of the propaganda surrounding the war. She will 'hold the fort' at home, which she makes 'sound the more heroic option' (p.57).

There is great poignancy at the end of this chapter when, despite talking up the adventure of Jim's departure, his father is left alone and is uncharacteristically affectionate. It is this that makes Jim 'for a moment, see things differently' (p.58) and recognise that his life was now to be forever changed.

Chapter 9 (pp.59–65)

In the same way that the opening chapter set the tone for the first part of the novel, so too this chapter introduces all the elements of the second part: the war with its violence, destruction and waste of young lives – the flipside.

Key scenes

Note Jim's state: he 'arrived at the dark side of his head, and got stuck there' (p.59); Clancy introduced (p.59); Bobby Cleese and tales of whiting (pp.60–1); how birds keep the parts of Jim's life connected (p.62); Jim 'picked' by Wizzer Green (pp.64–5).

The beauty, peace and familiarity of Jim's world at home are replaced by the ugliness and brutality of the alien world of war. These two sides of human existence are locked in battle with each other it seems, their struggle captured in Jim himself, who uses the birds to help him 'make a map in his head of how the parts of his life were connected' (p.62) while at the same time being confronted with 'some depth in himself ... that frightened him and which he did not understand' (p.65).

Among the many thousands of ordinary young men, he finds Clancy Parkett who, while very different from Jim, is 'someone he wouldn't want to be without' (p.60). Clancy tells stories that make him feel at home, that keep 'the old life real' (p.60). It is the same with Bobby Cleese, whose stories of fishing and Deception Bay are so vivid that the 'Whiting, thousands of them, were swarming under the blue surface of Bob Cleese's eyes' (p.62). Although he wants to speak about the swampland, Jim feels 'he had no stories of his own to relate' (p.60). Above all, it is the presence of the birds that connects him most strongly with his former life and convinces him in a way that he is still alive.

Despite the mud and death, nature survives and beauty still exists. The rich and detailed description of the birdlife Jim observes (pp.62–3) is testament to this. Still connected with his work at home, he records what he sees to report later to Imogen.

Enter Wizzer Green to destroy Jim's tenuous link with the other side of his life. The instant and intense dislike they have for each other shocks Jim and the reader. Jim realises he has to defend 'whatever it was in him that Wizzer rejected', but in doing so he discovers an aspect of himself he hasn't known and doesn't particularly like – 'the black anger', the 'murder in their eyes' (p.64). It is Clancy who steps in and gets a black eye for his trouble but neither Jim nor anyone else believes he has wimped out and let his mate take the fall for him. All recognise that he has been 'ready even to kill' (p.65). 'Enemies, like friends, told you who you were' (p.64) Jim decides: again, the two sides of the coin revealing the whole picture.

Chapter 10 (pp.66–70)

This and the next chapters are primarily concerned with setting the scene of the war experience for Jim and his friends and establishing the context in which Clancy's death occurs in Chapter 12.

Key scenes

Jim and Clancy race the train to get boiling water for their billy tea (pp.67–8); Jim is reminded of the building of the Pyramids (p.69).

After weeks of frustration doing nothing the young soldiers are relieved to be on the move, even though this means being transported in cattle trucks. Suitable for '*eight horses or forty men*' (p.66), the trucks were previously used to take animals to their slaughter.

While the irony is clear, the men at this stage don't feel the 'dumb terror' of the animals, still sufficiently naive to be looking forward to their arrival at the front. Remember that they are from Australia. They have travelled greater distances than they ever imagined possible. They have met many people, heard new languages, eaten strange food and all the time they have continued to believe, by and large, that they are involved in the ultimate battle between good and evil.

The business of war is depicted as complex and quite sophisticated. The scene at the front reminds Jim of a picture of the building of the Pyramids – those enduring symbols of early civilisation – he recalls from his childhood (see p.69). He is struck by the 'vast numbers of men engaged in an endeavour' (p.70) and is charmed by the fact that he, Jim Saddler from Queensland, is about to become a part of it.

Despite his exposure to the hardships of the war and the chilling confrontation with Wizzer Green, Jim remains the innocent young man. This is very clear in his and Clancy's boyish game to get some boiling water for tea from their train driver. He enjoys racing the train and the cheering of his comrades. The billy of water is held aloft 'as if it were some sort of trophy' (p.68) and he is thrilled that, though he would never have done it on his own, here now is a story he might tell others. Indeed, having Clancy with him makes it even more of an adventure. The tea, 'in sweet, steamy mouthfuls' (p.68), tastes as good as lollies, acquired surreptitiously, might to children.

Chapter 11 (pp.71–7)

Although 'Jim still existed in a world of his own, not withdrawn exactly but impenetrably private' (pp.72–3), he is being drawn inexorably into the war's vortex and this chapter takes him a step further.

Key scenes

Jim's first direct war experience in Armentières where people are distrustful of them although they are there to defend them (pp.71–2); Clancy persuades Jim to bend the rules a little and visit Monique's 'good estaminet' – a small cafe (p.75); Clancy confides in Jim about Margaret, the girl who 'knocked him back' and led to his joining up (p.76).

In Armentières, where Jim's company is billeted, the people of the area continue to try to go about their lives as normally as possible. Businesses continue in the town, particularly those that will be supported by the soldiers – cafes, brothels – and on the outskirts crops are grown alongside the trenches. The reader is reminded that these are ordinary people, like Jim and his friends, whose lives have been turned upside down. They are dubious about the defenders of their land and most of all 'just wanted the war to move away' (p.71). Many feel as invaded by the 'defenders' as by the enemy because they were 'always on the look out for something to eat or steal' (p.72).

After much urging from Clancy and despite his own reservations, Jim joins his friend on a Christmas visit to one of the women on Clancy's 'List'. He finally relents because 'it was, after all, their last night and the immediate future was unpredictable' (p.73). Unpredictable! Such understatement fails to capture the significance of his sentiments. Clancy presents the situation more accurately: when trying to stir the drunken young Eric he says, 'At least ... if he's goin' t' get killed f' Christmas he'll'v been pissed once in his life' (p.77).

A more important outcome of the visit is Clancy's telling of the story of Margaret, the woman who 'Knocked me back' (p.76). Jim is very unsettled by such revelation: 'He wasn't used to this sort of thing' (p.76). The plain, self-effacing, typically unemotional male Jim is stunned by Clancy's invitation to share his emotional life and the obvious link between Clancy's joining up and his rejection by a woman he clearly loved. Living on the edge of existence has had many consequences.

Chapter 12 (pp.78–90)

Finally they are at the front: the trenches and the daily existence of the soldiers are described in detail. There is no fighting. At first it is more a battle for survival against the elements, 'like some crazy camping trip under nightmare conditions', but then the 'invisible enemy' strikes (p.84).

Key scenes

A corpse hurls itself upon Jim (p.83); Clancy's death (p.86); Jim visits Eric in hospital (pp.87–8).

Getting to their position in the first place is a struggle, filing through the trenches, unable to stop for fear that 'the whole troop might take a wrong turning and be lost in the dark' (p.80) – as Jim feels he has done in his head. On their way they meet those who they are to replace and it seems that there are worse things than dying. Their unwashed bodies 'smelled like corpses' and 'in their heavy-eyed weariness' (p.80) it seems that the war has immediately transformed them into something not quite human. Or is their beaten look a dimension of human existence Jim is about to encounter?

For most of the eleven days at the front they confront many enemies other than the Germans. There is the smell, the endless foul water, the cold and the rats. Death is all around them and the water and the rats emphasise this. Walls collapse because of the 'stinking water that seeped endlessly out of the walls' (p.82), revealing rotting bodies that inhabit Jim's nightmares. The 'field-grey' rats 'burrowing right into a man's guts or tumbling about in dozens in the bellies of horses' (p.83) are creatures of the underworld for Jim, the flipside of the birds that 'were of life and the air' (p.84). It seems that Jim has indeed descended into hell.

Clancy's death

Suddenly, revoltingly, the real enemy appears. Clancy is 'blasted out of existence' (p.86), reduced to blood and slime that drenches Jim. There is a final, cheerful image of Clancy with billy in hand and two mugs for him and Jim. There is a cosy, almost domestic quality to the scene, Jim busying himself with the bread and jam. Amidst the awfulness of trench life they have established their little 'family' protecting themselves and each other. The cruel randomness and astonishing violence of war is all captured in the blast that knocks the breath out of Jim, severs Eric's legs and destroys Clancy's body totally.

But it does more than just knock the breath out of Jim. Surprisingly, 'that was how the war first touched him' (p.87). Despite the privation and ugliness of the previous weeks he has resisted despair. Some part of his old self has remained untouched and unspoiled – innocent – until now. Clancy was someone who Jim did not want to be without, who confided in him in a way others did not. How was Jim to survive the horror and the emptiness that was left? 'The body's wholeness, Jim saw, was an image a man carried in his head. It might persist after the fact' (p.86). Clancy no longer exists in a physical sense but he will live on in Jim's mind, in his life.

Jim's visit to Eric in hospital

Jim's visit to Eric signals the physical and emotional consequences of war for the young Australian soldiers and the loss of Jim's 'innocence'. Feeling guilty about young Eric's awful physical injuries when he himself is 'quite unharmed' (p.86), Jim goes to visit him in the hospital. Eric's truly pathetic situation as an orphan and now a cripple – who will look after him? – anticipates the circumstances in which many returned soldiers found themselves in the postwar years in Australia. Jim reassures him but his guilty acknowledgement that he will not make a return visit because 'It was Eric's questions he would be unable to face' (p.90) confirm the young man's prescience. Jim is left to weep harsh tears over which he has no control. He has no map in his head for what is happening to him.

Chapter 13 (pp.91–105)

Jim has now been at war for a long time – perhaps a year – and has survived against the odds. Unlike the previous chapter, Chapter 13 contains a great deal of imagery of warfare and its horrors.

Key scenes

Jim and Wizzer's encounter in the shellhole (pp.91–4); Bobby Cleese's death (pp.99–100); the discovery of the mammoth's remains (p.102).

Throughout this chapter the war imagery is graphic. There is the noise, the flashes of light, the ever-present danger, the presence of the enemy.

Jim is much changed, stripped of his emotional life by the brutality that surrounds him. The description of the men making their way through the lines (p.91) is reminiscent of that of the rats in the previous chapter. There is not much difference between the two, it now seems. Jim, like the rest, has 'stopped being scared of the dead' (p.91) but it is the 'sense of being alone out here that had broken him' (p.92).

Jim's encounter with Wizzer

Taking refuge in a shellhole after he 'decided then that he'd had enough' (p.92), Jim has a strange encounter with Wizzer, his alter ego whose revelations about himself so frightened Jim when he first arrived. Their original fight seems destined to continue at first when Wizzer attacks Jim, obviously thinking him the enemy. 'A friend!' (p.90) Jim exclaims ironically. The exchange that follows completes their interaction. Alarmed that 'in [Wizzer's] own frank admission of cowardice that they were two of a kind' (p.94), Jim suddenly wants to be back in the field, 'Scared silly, but not sullied' (p.95). The experience leaves him so afraid, so aware of the dark side of his head, that he no longer hears the deafening noise of battle close by. But Jim's refusal to collude precipitates a complete emotional collapse in Wizzer. He dissolves into wracking sobs and is paralysed with fear. Despite Jim's encouragement, Wizzer is unable to leave the shellhole and Jim is forced to leave him alone, presumably to die. He rejoins the battle and finds Bobby Cleese, grateful that 'he wasn't lost after all' (p.96).

The 'unfairness' of war

Thus hurled back into the chaos of battle, Jim is under the command of an officer, no more than a boy who seems to have learned his part from reading *Chums*, a boy's own journal full of tales of heroism and 'boyish nobility' (p.98). The look in his eyes when hit suggests to Jim a sense of 'I wasn't ready. Unfair!' (p.98). He expresses the feelings of all the young men for whom life has 'declare[d] itself' (p.97) in this way. Of course they are not ready. None of it is fair but they nonetheless 'rose up on a signal and poured into it ... the mouth of hell' (p.100).

Bobby Cleese's death; the discovery of the mammoth's remains

'Bob Cleese got a bad dose [of the gas phosgene] but didn't die till two days later' (p.100). Jim gets permission to visit him. On the way he meets the group of soldiers who have been 'mining' and have discovered the fossilised remains of a mammoth. It is a profound and moving discovery that places the horror of wartime experience into a broader context – that of the long history of life on earth.

Key quote

> ... even here among the horrors of battle a spirit of scientific enquiry could be pursued, its interests standing over and above the particular circumstances of war ... (p.103)

For Jim, time is made meaningless by the sight of the discovery. These feelings are added to by Bobby's horrible death (p.100) and the experience of witnessing all the men he sees come and go 'like living through whole generations' (p.104).

Chapter 14 (pp.106–12)

Jim recognises that formerly 'he had been living ... in a state of dangerous innocence' (p.107) but finds hope when he sees an old man digging. He is then able to find order in the chaos and reconnection with his past through recording the birdlife of the area.

Key scenes

> Jim recollects the death of his fifteen-year-old brother who fell onto the blades of the harvester (p.107) and the cruelty a kestrel inflicted on him when he tried to free it (p.108); Jim responds to the old man digging rows in the 'utterly blasted ... field' (p.109); he recommences recording the birdlife (p.111).

Jim is slipping into despair, fearing, or perhaps believing, that the nightmare will go on forever: 'They had fallen, he and his contemporaries, into a dark pocket of time from which there was no escape' (p.107). It is the apparent endlessness of the war and the sense of 'what can ever stand against it?' (p.108) that so depress him, more so than the random violence or the terrible hardship. Two snippets from his earlier life underline this.

Jim's brother's death and the cruelty of the kestrel

Jim is acquainted with violence, shockingly so. Before his eyes, his little brother was cut to pieces falling off a harvester. A maimed kestrel tore Jim's hands as he worked to free it from the sardine tin tied to its leg. The detail of these two scenes is as vivid and gruesome as any of the war. So, it is not the violence alone that has sapped his energy and left him feeling that the life of the birds is no longer worth recording. It is 'the disintegrating power of that cruelty' (p.109) that has finally worn him down and wiped out his remembrance of the sanctuary at home and the rich resilience of the birds' kingdom.

The old man digging and memory of Miss Harcourt

An old man digging a vegetable plot and a memory of Miss Harcourt bring him back from the brink. It is a sign of the disintegration of things that the soldiers first think the man is digging a grave and then decide he is just crazy. For Jim it is 'his refusal to accept the limiting nature of conditions' (p.110) that reminds him of Imogen and leads him to return to his notes on the birds – 'to keep hold of himself and of the old life that he had come close to losing' (p.111).

Though he wonders occasionally if the old man's digging has produced beans or turnips, he never returns to the place and tellingly 'didn't even know where it was, since they never saw a map' (p.111).

Chapter 15 (pp.113–18)

Ashley Crowther returns to the story – as an officer his war experiences contrast with Jim's. The chapter focuses on Ashley's attitudes to war, his response to his men and how he finds the resolve to go on in the face of this seemingly endless war – drawing a parallel between his and Jim's experiences.

Key scenes

Man mending hoe (p.114); Ashley likens men to creatures killed when hunting (p.110); reflections on the soldier and the civilian (pp.116–17); Ashley's views on the long-term effects of the war (p.117).

Here, we share Ashley Crowther's viewpoint as he watches the men rest after a twelve-hour walk. He marvels at the men's power to endure and the army's 'awful wisdom in ... the logistics of battle and the precise breaking point of men' (p.114). Like the man planting the vegetable plot, there is a man mending a hoe who Ashley notices; Ashley is amazed by the possibility that this man might 'believe the coming battle was the end and that he might soon have need of the hoe' (p.114). Ashley, not so confident, is overwhelmed by a sense that 'Nothing after this would ever be the same ... maybe all life would be organised like war' (p.117). Weary that 'the deadly sewing-machines were stitching their shrouds' (p.115), his horror at the carnage takes him back to a hunting weekend when he was at Cambridge. The death of the soldiers in his command reminded him of 'watching the creatures spring up and turn somersaults in the air or roll away twitching' (p.115).

The men are like the birds at home – the way Jim and Ashley see them. They are part of an enormous throng, each in their uniform indistinguishable from the other – 'men', 'reinforcements', 'casualties' (p.117). But they have names like Snow, Skeeter and Tommo and they had 'their worlds, each one, about which [Ashley] could only guess' (p.115). Like the photo of the sandpiper that allows Jim to look for the first time *'into the creature's unique life'* (p.28), the war experience has captured the essence of the soldiers he is with and he can see that 'the civilian in these men survived' (p.116), the essential qualities that made them distinct and individual.

But Ashley has had a different war from Jim. He is an officer. His class and wealth determined this in the first place but he has found, to his surprise, that he has 'the lineaments of an officer. He was calm, he kept his head; he kept an eye out for his men; they trusted him' (p.117). He is also aware that he has been lucky, like Jim, to survive. But how lucky are they really? How well will they 'survive'? What if 'it' – the war, the destruction, the dark side – continues until all is lost? Ashley cannot see an end in sight because perhaps from now on 'all life would be organised like war' (p.117) which would mean that this battle would be only a stage in an endless process. This thought and that the process must be resisted ultimately gives him his resolve: 'It seemed more important than ever now to hang on ... and if his luck held, to go back' (p.118).

Chapter 16 (pp.119–24)

The writing develops a surreal quality in this and the next chapter as Malouf depicts the storm in Jim's tormented mind and then conveys the peace that death finally brings.

Key scene

Jim is strangely detached from himself and the war and experiences an almost transcendent overview of the activities of life; his mental map is 'immensely expanded' (pp.122–4).

Jim prepares to go over the top once again, but this time he seems to know that it will be the last time. As he and his comrades wait for what must be certain death they become overwhelmed by their own bodies. They had 'gone deep inside themselves and were coming to terms with the blood as it rolled round and round from skull to foot, still miraculously flowing in its old course' (p.120). They fight fear and find resolve: *'No, I am not going to die'* (p.121). Jim is entirely at one with his fellow soldiers here; they are united, their experience a singular one.

Jim is acutely aware of the roughness of his uniform and the weight of his pack and yet, as the whistle blows and he launches himself out of the trench, he feels 'out of himself and floating' (p.122). In the last moments before being hit he does take on the nature of a bird. Though he moves across the ground he sees things from above 'as it might look from Bert's bi-plane' (p.122). He can see it all – the lines of trenches, the machine guns, the men running, killing and being killed. But he also sees the woodlice, a snail, a bird or two 'like the couple of wheatears he had seen once in a field much like this' (p.123), and his trance-like state moves from the misery and fear of the battlefield to the beauty and triumph of nature. The continuum of life is thus reaffirmed. In all this he sees 'his own life, neither more nor less important than the rest ... but unique because it was his head that contained it' (p.123). Indeed, Jim is astonished that his mental map has 'so immensely expanded' (p.124) and so he reaches heights of awareness previously unknown to him.

Chapter 17 (pp.125–36)

Jim, seriously injured, finds himself in the tent hospital with Ashley. He moves between life and death, experiencing a vision of dead soldiers.

Key scenes

Jim's injury (pp.125–7); his meeting with Ashley Crowther in the tent hospital (p.129); his recollections of Ashley's acute response to the band music (p.129) and later his playing of the piano at the chateau (pp.130–1); Jim's death experience (pp.134–6).

Jim is injured badly and obviously loses a great deal of blood. As life seeps out of him he can feel 'the coarsening of the grains out of which his flesh was composed ... as first his hand dissolved, then his arm, then his shoulder' (p.126). In a light moment he reflects wryly that there'll be nothing of him for the stretcher-bearers to collect 'if things [go] on like this' (p.126). Remembering his emergency field dressing he thinks about how he might use it, how it might stretch back 'To the Coast. To home' (p.128) it is so long. Then he slips into unconsciousness.

Waking in a hospital tent he recognises his predicament. It is very quiet and the place is full of men 'maimed and crudely bandaged' who have 'given themselves up utterly to a process of slow dissolution' (p.127). Although his instinct still says '*I am in the wrong place ... I don't belong here*' (p.127) he knows nonetheless that 'the look on his face must be the same look these other faces wore, anxious, submissive' (p.128). And so it will end for him and all the other young Australians. Jim is struck by how predetermined is their fate, their whole lives somehow directed towards this moment – 'they had spent their whole life thus, a foot from the block and waiting, even in the safe city streets and country yards, even at home in Australia' (p.128).

Jim recognises Ashley and recollects two previous meetings

Suddenly he hears a familiar voice – Ashley Crowther's. He is astonished to find him here, 'also in the shambles' (p.129). Somehow, it seemed Ashley would escape all this. Jim thinks about the last two occasions that he has seen his friend. Both involve music. In the first, Ashley's keen sense of music alerts Jim to a distant band playing above the din of enemy fire. In the second, his playing of a piano 'might have been taken over from the nightingale's song and elaborated ... The music was neither gay nor sad ... it was like the language, beyond known speech, that birds use' (p.131). So, nearing death, Jim is not only united with Ashley but also reconnected with his life in the sanctuary and its sense of balance and rightness. It is a different Jim, changed forever by his experiences, but Jim nonetheless, able to reach out now and comprehend the birds' language 'and if he did, however briefly, much would become clear to him that would otherwise stay hidden' (p.131).

Jim's death

Writers have long been interested in the death experience. There are the last moments of consciousness and then what? Malouf offers his ideas here in his depiction of Jim's death. Jim moves into a dreamlike state but only slowly does it become apparent that he has moved beyond reality. Though mortally wounded, he and Ashley get up from their beds, walk past doctors and nurses and out of the tent towards a moonlit wood. As it becomes light and the birds start singing he recognises the place as the one where he had seen the old man digging – the place he thought he would not return to because he did not have a map. The blasted trees are renewed, birds sing, potatoes grow in neat rows. And there are men digging. He happily joins them enjoying the smell of the earth which has 'a smell that belonged to the beginning of things' (p.134).

Ashley has disappeared but who does he meet? Clancy, who, he says, did not disappear into thin air: 'Not air, mate. Earth'. At first dubious about Clancy's claim of 'digging through to the other side', he is convinced by the numbers of men doing it, 'hundreds of men, all caked with mud, long-haired, bearded, in ragged uniforms' (p.135), men just like him, and grinning at his friend, he joins in. There is both tragedy and triumph. While the image the reader is left with might suggest the men are just digging their own graves, the digging is a liberating experience for Jim because he sees that this is 'what hands were intended for, this steady digging into the earth, as wings were meant for flying over the curve of the planet to another season' (p.136).

Chapter 18 (pp.137–42)

We return to Imogen Harcourt in Australia and her coming to terms with Jim's death.

Key scenes

Imogen's reaction to Jim's father's responses to his son's death (pp.138–9); Imogen's responses to Jim's death (pp.139–40); the surfer (p.141); her sense of the new and things changed (pp.141–2).

Back in Australia, the natural world is untouched by the ravages of war. The 'intense activity and endless change' (p.137) of the sea, the beach, the birds, the seasons continuing. But things have changed. Jim is dead and Imogen is left alone, with a grief that is beyond her experience and comprehension. Their brief friendship somehow denies her the right to express her loss openly as his father can. Yet for two days 'she had been unable to move ... the waste of it [has] torn at her breast' (pp.139–40) and now she just sits repeating his name, trying to make sense of his life and death and what it meant to her. She recognises that Jim's lonely, hurt and angry father should perhaps share his grief in order to 'let Jim, now that he was dead, back into his life' (p.139) as she must if she is to come to terms with her loss.

Watching a surfer ride waves on a board, something she has never seen before, something symbolic of the new postwar world, Imogen comes to a crucial realisation – 'A life wasn't *for* anything. It simply was' (p.140). She has an acute vision of Jim as he gazed at her photos of the sandpiper. His image was 'just then so very like the birds, alert, unique, utterly present' (p.140). Her new understanding is like Jim's when Clancy dies – that a person lives on in the mind of another who loves them. It is the life itself that is precious and complete, however long or short, unique and 'essential in every creature' (p.140). Jim's ordinary life is thus celebrated for the uniqueness that lies at the heart of human existence and transcends 'birth, position, talent even' (p.140).

Imogen is a lonely figure as she leaves the beach, comforted somewhat by her new knowledge but in pain still. She is attracted to the idea of photographing the young surfer even though 'This eager turning, for a moment, to the future, surprised and hurt her' (p.142). And before she loses sight of him altogether she turns and looks again, wanting the optimism of the 'brilliant balance up there' (p.142).

CHARACTERS & RELATIONSHIPS

Jim Saddler

Jim is the vehicle for Malouf's exploration of life and its meaning. He is the key to the whole work, all other characters being drawn in terms of their relationship with him. His journey from innocence is not easy – can it ever be? Through painful and horrifying ordeals he finally emerges anew. Positive in his outlook on life, he no longer fears death because he values life for its moment and not for what might be.

What sort of person is Jim? It has been said many times that he is an 'ordinary man'. But what does this mean? In the context of the story it means he is a working-class, first- or second-generation Australian. He has modest expectations of life and of the relationships he forms. He expects to live and die where he has been born and raised – on the south coast of Queensland. All this makes him ordinary. But from the outset, it is also clear that being 'ordinary' doesn't mean that he is like everyone else. His interest in the birds, his ability to form relationships with two unlikely companions – Ashley and Imogen – immediately identify him as unique, as each of his birds is unique. Then, extraordinary things happen to him and he becomes the embodiment of the human condition. Content and asking little of life he might be, but it is only in the darkness of war, the hell of evil and destruction which he finds himself in, that he understands himself fully and accepts who he is – both the light and dark sides.

In his actions and attitudes when in the war, Jim continues to be the 'ordinary man', self-effacing, shy and humble. Though he'd like to, he doesn't have the confidence to share stories of home the way mates like Clancy and Bobby do (pp.61–2). Chasing the train with Clancy to secure some boiling water for tea from its driver gives him a sense that maybe this was a story he could tell (p.68). But it is crucial that the experience is shared with Clancy. Had he been alone, he wouldn't have thought it worth telling. Jim is not someone who would be noticed much in a crowd.

Yet it is he that Malouf has chosen to convey the dark recesses of the human mind as well as the glorious flight of the human spirit.

Jim's encounters with Wizzer are central to an understanding of the 'innocence to experience' journey Malouf takes Jim on. Their first meeting catapults Jim into a new and sudden realisation of self as well as the murderous contest. He sees himself anew through his enemy and recognises painfully the part of himself he has suppressed – 'Enemies, like friends, told you who you were' (p.64). Both sides are needed in order for the picture to be complete. When they meet again in the shellhole they are locked together once again, first in battle and then in the struggle to survive. Jim is again confronted by the 'dark side' but this time he is the stronger, both physically and emotionally. Although drawn briefly to the abyss of Wizzer's despair, he steps back from it. He escapes the emotional destruction of the shellhole and chooses to return to the battlefield, his choking fear conquered.

Before he leaves Australia for the war Jim acknowledges that his life will be changed forever. What does the war do to Jim? With the knowledge of his traumatic experiences there and his ultimate death it seems just too trite say that it changes him. Malouf is saying something more than this about him. Rather than change him, the war completed Jim. It is the fully human Jim – whose painful self-knowledge includes an awareness of his own weakness, his capacity for violence and the limitations of his relationships hitherto – who is mourned at the end of the novel, his 'dangerous innocence' (p.107) destroyed but his integrity and uniqueness intact.

The maps in Jim's head

References to the maps in Jim's head occur at the following points. Each should be looked at carefully and considered in the light of his journey.

- Chapter 1, p.2: 'He had a map of all this clearly in his head ... He moved always on these two levels, through these two worlds: the flat world of individual grassblades, seen so close up they blurred ... and the long view in which all this part of the country was laid out like a relief map in the Shire office'.

- Chapter 2, pp.20–1: 'It amazed him, this. That he could be watching ... a creature that only weeks ago had been on the other side of the earth and had found its way here ... without a single guiding mark ... Did it know where it had arrived on the earth's surface? Did it retain, in that small eye, some image of the larger world ...?'
- Chapter 8, pp.54–5: When Jim goes up in Ashley's plane 'what came to him most clearly was how the map in his own head ... might be related to the one the birds carried in theirs'. The flight gives him 'a new view after all'. He later thinks of this 'as his last vision of the world he knew'.
- Chapter 9, p.61: Jim is now at the war and Bob Cleese is sharing stories of the thousands of whiting at Deception Bay. While this helps the men cope with the appalling conditions, Jim realises that there is something 'more reassuring than ... the places, the stories of a life that was continuous elsewhere'. A 'kind of private reassurance for himself alone, was the presence of the birds, that allowed Jim to make a map in his head of how the parts of life were connected, there and here, and to find his way back at times to a natural cycle of things that the birds still followed undisturbed'.
- Chapter 16, pp.122–3: 'he was ... seeing the scene ... as it might look from Bert's bi-plane, remote and silent. Perhaps he had ... taken on the nature of a bird; though it was with a human eye that he saw, and his body, still entirely his own, was lumbering along below ... in a breathless dream of black hail striking all about him.' (Note this key section continues through to the end of the chapter when he realises that his mental map has 'immensely expanded'.)

The map as a metaphor

The idea of the map operates as metaphor for Jim searching for selfhood and his place in the world. But the device also works to connect Jim very closely with the birds he so admires and loves.

Though he has little experience of life, Jim carries a map in his head of the world around him. It is the same map he thinks that the birds carry, the same map that allows them to navigate their way halfway across the world and to find 'their' place on the other side. It is thus very important to him that he can retain these maps. Without them, presumably, he would be lost. And lost he is, when he goes to the 'other side'. He cannot find his place. He is, like the dunlin, a refugee in an alien world. However, while closely connected with the birds, Jim is not of them. He is other. He cannot migrate so successfully to the other side of the world, or of his head, from paradise to hell. There are no maps for this. Significantly, when he is dying he reconnects with the birds, his home and his past. Before he dies he has a vision of the overall pattern of life – one that incorporates him into life with its war and destruction and the domestic, the ordinary, the humble and the innocent. What finally astonishes him is that the map in his head has 'immensely expanded' (p.124), enabling him to reconcile the innocence and the cruelty of life and to accept that 'his own life was neither more nor less important than the rest' (p.123).

Point of view

All the other characters in the book are seen mainly through Jim's eyes. (In Chapter 15 the reader shares Ashley's viewpoint; similarly, the final chapter presents Imogen's viewpoint as we enter into her thoughts on Jim's death.) Nevertheless, Jim is the linchpin of the text and source of most of the reader's knowledge of Ashley, Imogen and the rest. These two in particular emerge nonetheless as significant characters and deserve individual and careful examination.

Ashley Crowther

Ashley and Jim's friendship is an unlikely partnership. Despite their very different personalities and vastly different backgrounds there is a meeting of minds between the two young men from the time of their first encounter that transcends class and education. Ashley is also of spiritual and historical significance in the novel.

Ashley and Jim have a shared interest in the birds but their relationship is much deeper. They have a respect for the world around them in a way that many do not. Much of what they share is in silence and this is surely a mark of the deep and abiding contact each makes with the other. Ashley gives Jim the opportunity to do what he has always wanted to do. Jim provides Ashley with The Book. In the end, it is Ashley who appears as Jim is dying and who accompanies him on his last journey.

Ashley, though not as obviously typical as Jim, is a very Australian young man. Born in Australia, he nonetheless has spent time in England, becoming the young gentleman his class expects him to be. But the attitudes and behaviour of the upper class have begun to mutate in the Australian experience. Ashley presides over his land like a traditional squire, yet he has a respect for and connection with the land that acknowledges its age. Despite resistance from some of his contemporaries in England to the idea of living in Australia, he regards it as his home because it is 'closest to the centre of his being' (p.11). His respect for the land and recognition of its integrity and long life is remarkable and suggests a sensitivity to Aboriginal notions of custodianship of and belonging to the land.

His relationship with Jim is the key, of course. Ashley and Jim would not have forged such a close bond had he not been a bit different, not consistent with all the expectations of an upper-class man of his time, not stereotypical. After he and Jim both go off to war, he does not appear again until Chapter 15. As an officer he has had a different, marginally more comfortable war than Jim, but what is striking when he resurfaces is the continuing similarities in their thoughts of what has happened to the world and the strategies they use to maintain their sanity. Each is overwhelmed by the prospect that the war, in some form, will go on forever, but seeks comfort from and reassurance in nature. Ashley however does not seem as prone to despair as Jim. As an officer he is buoyed by his role, comforted by the satisfaction that leadership gives him and the meaning this gives to what he is doing. Jim has no such succour.

Jim's two meetings with Ashley during the war are described in Chapter 17 and deserve close examination. Both relate to music that is in turn connected to birdsong. In the second episode, the singing of a young boy and the singing of the nightingales almost become one and when Jim hears the piano playing a little later it 'might have been taken over from the nightingale's song and elaborated, all tender trills' (p.131). It is Ashley playing the piano, brought down from the ruined, abandoned chateau nearby. Jim is astonished by how much Ashley has changed – 'his whole body ... came to a kind of attention Jim had not seen there on previous occasions' (p.132). The suggestion is that Ashley too is now more complete, rather than changed. Like Jim, his experience of the war, though terrible, has allowed him to understand his own life and its meaning more fully and to recognise that 'There were so many worlds. They were all continuous with one another and went on simultaneously' (p.115).

Ashley is there when Jim dies. Malouf intentionally obscures the moment of Jim's death but whether it is in reality or dream, Ashley is there. It is he who goes with Jim out to the field to meet Clancy and then disappears. This was a true friendship, deep, abiding and transformative. Jim will live on through Ashley because his was 'an image a man carried in his head' (p.86).

Imogen Harcourt

Like Ashley, the character of Imogen Harcourt, though briefly drawn, is vibrant and real and crucial to the success of the novel.

Imogen is the mildly eccentric single woman who has subsumed any desires she may have had for relationships and conventional life in her passion for photography and wildlife. Her photos have great impact on Jim and augment his ability to observe the birds. But Imogen's role is more than just to do this. It is notable that the novel concludes with her and it is her tortured realisation of the meaning of Jim's life and death that provides the optimism at the end, without which the reader, like Jim, would be drawn towards despair.

All the other women referred to the novel – there are no other real female characters – are profoundly stereotypical. They are wives, excitable girls who are free with their sexual favours or whores. Without the interesting and challenging character of Imogen, the story would be subject to justifiable feminist criticism. But Imogen is a complex individual, both a character who belongs to her own times and an enduring model of a woman who creates a life for herself, accepting the compromises this entails.

It is worth developing a brief biography of Imogen. In the early part of the century she has travelled to Australia with a brother who, like many, is seeking to make good in the new land. The brother's hopes are not fulfilled and he returns to Norfolk, but Imogen decides to stay. She supplements her small income with photos for a London magazine and lives alone in the not always hospitable Australian bush. Many would find such an odyssey difficult today, let alone eighty years ago when the likes of Ashley's friends regarded Australia as a rather barbarian frontier land. But Imogen, Jim discovers straight away, is not like other women who 'tried harder to please' (p.26). She is a person who is in touch with her emotions, but doesn't succumb to them. The appearance of the sandpiper reminds her of Norfolk and makes her homesick. She readily acknowledges this, but 'set up quickly, got a good shot, and there it is. Homesickness dealt with. Stuffed into the box' (p.27). Others resent her strength of character and self-possession – 'she had her own rules and kept them but didn't care for other people's' (p.47) – and found her 'as a subject for gossip, unmanageable, unrewarding' (p.48).

Imogen is the only character who questions the war and Australia's participation in it. She is angry that Jim is going, regarding it as stupid rather than heroic, but accepts it nonetheless and is the one who sees him off. While she is unable to influence his decision, it is she who, in some ways, saves him in the end – not from death but from desolation. Long months in the trenches bring Jim to the point of giving up, both physically and emotionally, but the sight of an old man preparing a vegetable garden renews his faith. What strikes him most and reminds him of Imogen is the old man's 'refusal to accept the limiting nature of conditions' (p.110). This captures the essence of Imogen's life, the choices she has made and what she means to Jim. She is not limited by her gender, by the physically harsh Australian environment, by social expectations. She is quite simply just herself. It this insight into her that allows the reader to see '*into the creature's unique life*' (p.28) as her photos do for Jim with the birds.

Despite the brief time they have spent together, Imogen's grief at Jim's death reflects the strength of the connection between them and the extent to which they have revealed themselves to each other. Imogen is overwhelmed but also confused by the anguish she feels. It is not just that she will miss him, that the happiness of their common work has been cut short. It is that Jim's life has been wasted. What was it all *for*, she continues to ask herself. Unless this question is answered satisfactorily, the reader too must feel dissatisfied, but it is through Imogen that the answer comes:

> That is what life meant, a unique presence, and it was essential in every creature. To set anything above it, birth, position, talent even, was to deny to all but a few among the infinite millions what was common and real, and what was also, in the end, most moving. A life wasn't *for* anything. It simply was. (p.140)

Thus captured in her mind, like the birds in the photos or recorded in The Book, Jim transcends death and lives on – still a part of the continuum of life.

The book closes with Imogen standing alone on the beach, turning for another look at the waves and the surfer riding them, drawn by his optimism.

Jim's father

He appears only briefly on three occasions but Jim's father, whose name is never even revealed, is a tragic figure who adds to the understanding of Jim and who fills out the picture of the Australia of the times.

The 'baleful look [Jim's] father turned on the world had no reason, it simply was' (p.6). He could not be more unlike Jim. His father, it is acknowledged, has had a hard life: sent out to work at age ten, he has lost a child and then his wife. He expects nothing more than the 'flat' life he believes he and 'the likes of us' (p.5) are destined for – poor, working men of rural Australia. But this doesn't fully explain the baleful (menacing) look. There is something fundamentally malevolent about him, which frightens Jim and which he seeks to avoid so as not to be 'infected' (p.6). It is in him that Jim subconsciously sees his own dark side reflected, sees what is revealed to him so brutally later on in his contact with Wizzer.

The father's view of the world seems to be confirmed in Jim's wartime experience and his subsequent death. The grief Imogen witnesses is not based on shock or the emptiness of loss but on an awful acceptance that his pernicious view has been a correct one. He doesn't want sympathy. Rather, he wants to extend his hatred for others further; he feels more justified than ever in his view of the world. There is no room for optimism here. There is also no room for emotional release or recovery. Imogen wonders if sharing her grief with Jim's father might 'offer him some release from himself and to let Jim, now that he was dead, back into his life' (p.139). He did, in fact, let his son back into his life, however briefly, when Jim left for the war. The unusual gesture of putting his hand on the back of the soon-to-be soldier's newly shaved head gives a momentary insight into what might have been. The gesture is such a surprise that Jim realises after this that his life will never be the same. But it is only in the context of Jim's departure that the brief affection can be displayed, and thus it is an ending, not a beginning.

Jim and his father are, of course, the two sides of the same coin – binary opposites – as with all things, so Malouf is saying. It is not remarkable that the gentle, shy, nature-sensitive Jim is the son of the cold, savage, dismissive father; it is normal. The tragedy for the father is that he is unwilling to expose his other side and nothing happens to force it. Not so with Jim. It is his journey to the other side that completes him, makes him fully human and allows him to die peacefully.

Clancy Parkett

Jim and Clancy's friendship – mateship – is a key element in the Anzac legend and this is a significant part of Clancy's role in the novel.

Clancy Parkett is a man who, though very unlike Jim, is recognised immediately by Jim as 'someone he wouldn't want to be without' (p.60). This bond speaks of the communication that is possible from first contact and of the wonder at how life could have been normal without that person up to this point. Such is the relationship between Jim and Clancy.

When Australian wartime memories are talked or written about, regardless of where the action took place, the common theme is always mateship. When asked to talk about their war experience, men and women will nearly always talk about their friends and, in the worst case, how the loss of friends was the most frightening and devastating thing that happened to them. This is how it is for Jim and Clancy and this is Malouf's purpose in presenting this short but central relationship. Their bond represents all those bonds between men in the trenches; their happy communion only seconds before Clancy's death is a symbol of what such friendship can do for people in adversity. Eric, Bobby and even Wizzer all add to the picture.

Clancy is, in fact, an almost stereotypical Australian 'bloke' of his time. He has the larrikin qualities Australian soldiers became famous for. He likes liquor and women and to flout the law. Jim couldn't be more unlike him. Yet it is Clancy who teaches Jim about the sharing of emotional pain, something Jim finds difficult. Clancy's story about Margaret, the woman he loved and lost, challenges Jim's idea of how male friends communicate and what they talk about. It is the probable imminence of death that precipitates the confession, such confidences being very out of character for the normally lighthearted Clancy, but it reveals a more complete picture of Jim's friend, and makes his death in the next chapter all the more shocking and sad.

Wizzer

Wizzer is worth some consideration. He is only revealed through his antipathy for Jim. How remarkable he is, though, as result. How could anyone react so negatively, and so instantly, to Jim – gentle, modest, undemanding Jim. It is these very qualities, it is suggested, that arouse the animosity. In the same way that Wizzer confronts Jim with his dark side, perhaps it is the good in Jim that so affronts and frightens Wizzer, recognising the challenge to find the good in himself.

To some extent Wizzer also represents the elements of Jim's father that Jim must confront. Later, when he meets Wizzer in the shellhole, Jim is fleetingly tempted to join Wizzer in his instinctive desire to abandon the war. Jim, however, overcomes the moment and recognises that he must resume his responsibilities and return to the fighting. He really wants Wizzer to accompany him – partly out of fear, it is true, but perhaps also because he recognises at some level that Wizzer has sunk into a more primitive state, and needs Jim's assistance if he is to reclaim his dignity and humanity.

Bob Cleese and Eric

Bobby and Eric are minor symbols of the mass of young men who went to the war and either died or came back horribly maimed. They do little of significance beyond this. It is notable however that Jim visits both in their hospital beds, is overwhelmed by the awfulness of their situations and falsely agrees to visit them again, while admitting to himself that he will not. Jim is not without obvious flaws. These two incidents convey his weakness in this regard – an understandable one but a weakness nonetheless. He teaches himself to endure the daily grind of trench life but he cannot endure the suffering and anguish of his friends.

THEMES, IDEAS & VALUES

Binary opposites

As has already been noted, Malouf is seriously interested in the two sides of all things. Innocence and experience is the major example he explores, but there are many others. There are the two sides of the world, north and south, old and new, sophisticated and crude, past and present, war-torn and peaceful. There are two sides to life, the most obvious being life and death but in addition there are ignorance and knowledge, happiness and sorrow, youth and age, love and hate. All these are represented in Jim and his relationships with others. The birdlife conveys migration and permanence, predator and prey, alien and familiar, individual and group identity. The two halves of the novel reflect the binary division that is being explored throughout. But the idea is conveyed most strongly through Jim's story and his acceptance of both the light and dark sides of life and of himself. It is a painful struggle and one that almost destroys him but which he survives, emotionally, and so can then die peacefully. Imogen, in her grief, comes to the realisation that Jim's seemingly wasted life did in fact have enduring meaning. This is precisely what Jim learns about himself when he faces the dark side and overcomes despair.

Innocence and experience

In Jim's journey from innocence, the innocence is blissful and the experience is horrifying, yet he emerges triumphant.

Clearly, without the searing experiences of war, Jim would not have grown in the way he did. Would he have been better off had he remained in innocence, or, as he says himself, was it dangerous? Are those who loved him better off for this 'growth'?

Malouf's answer is not that one is either good or bad or better than the other, but simply that they had to be. The innocence demanded the experience. Each made the other more pronounced, able to be seen in sharper relief. In Jim's case the two parts of his life are at opposite ends of the spectrum, the extremes of each circumstance. Of course it is not always so, but such contrast is used by Malouf to establish his point.

What is meant by Jim's 'innocence'? It doesn't mean a life without hardship. His childhood and early adulthood have been characterised by loss and emotional aridity. His mother and brother both died. His father provided him with little care or comfort. Until he meets Ashley it seems he has had few friends. He has no wealth and can look forward to a life of hard work to make a living. So what is it about Jim's life that makes him 'innocent'? The potential bleakness of his story is relieved by his skill and interest in birdwatching, and this holds the key to his state of mind. While he demands little of others and is content with his own company – apart from the birds – he still has a self-centred view of the world. He believes that though things may happen to him, he remains in control of his life, that it is his to determine. Despite the fact that he observes and marvels at the birds and recognises their individuality within the flock, he is unable to transfer this perception to himself. It is only the experience of the war that makes this happen.

It is not just the violence and brutalities of the war experience that transform Jim and his view of life. Although the physical shock is obviously very significant, it is his observation of others that allows him to 'recognise their individuality within the flock' and his interaction with particular men that confronts him with his whole self, enabling him to shed his 'innocence' with confidence.

Is a life incomplete without such a journey? *Fly Away Peter* says it is, but all journeys are not going to be the same and all people are not going to be as open as Jim is. In this way he is a truly noble character, an ordinary man without notable achievement who nonetheless conveys what it is to be fully human.

The individual

One of Malouf's main concerns is with the place of the individual within the wider pattern of existence. On the one hand there is the passing nature of Jim's life and youthful death. On the other hand the whole novel is about the place of each creature in a continuing evolving pattern. This is clear in all the descriptions of the birds, their appearance and their migration patterns. The identification of so many by name and where they have come from emphasises this. The metaphor is taken up in the chapters on the war. Initially the images are of overwhelming numbers swarming over the countryside without individual identity, just part of the war machine. However, personalities emerge – Clancy, Wizzer and later, through Ashley, many are named, in the same way the birds are named in the earlier chapters, the naming establishing the identity and the individuality.

In much of the story, however, there is an apparent randomness about the world which leads to the question, what does it all mean? How can one individual be of any significance? In Jim Saddler, Malouf has depicted the common man and eulogised him as noble and notable. Such is the value in every life. And so it must be. How can an individual love, strive, endure pain and disappointment if he or she sees themselves only as one speck in a myriad, random arrangement? Most importantly, the value of that life continues after the individual's death.

War

It has been said that this is an unusual war book in that it contains no real battles. A war book it is nonetheless, and a profound one at that. The lurid, awful detail of the trenches challenges all notions of the bravery and excitement that war is supposed to engender. The scenes at the front raise important questions about why people go to war, what is gained and what is lost. However, Malouf takes the study of war further than this. In defiance of the obscenity of war, nature seems relentless. Trees continue to blossom and bear fruit, farmers dig paddocks for planting, birds nest and fly and sing. This transcendence of horror empowers Jim and gives him the strength to rise above the battle at the end and to see it from outside as only one part of a much larger picture.

Other issues and ideas

Australia's history and identity

Remarkably, this short novel throws up many more ideas. Australia's history and identity are explored through the contrast between Jim's isolated naivety on the Queensland coast and his shocking thrust into the reality of the European war. The raw, still new country is symbolised thus. The classes are represented in Ashley and Jim and the continuing arrival of new people from the old world in Imogen – and of course the migratory birds.

Violence

Violence is a major theme. The novel's violence is both natural and created. There is the brutality of war, but the tranquil Australian bush is not without its violent side. The death of Jim's brother shows that. The gut-wrenching detail in which the harvester accident is described presses the point that violent death can occur at any time. Human beings are constantly threatened with dreadful annihilation. It is not just war that can take life without warning.

Land and territory

Land is an issue of great interest to Malouf. The 1914–18 war was about land and the desire to take it from others. The underlying attitude in wartime is that land is territory and as such becomes merely the object of political dispute and a symbol of victory when borders are moved and the size of the country increased. The reality of trench warfare was that each day thousands of lives were lost in order to gain a small amount of land from the enemy – which was usually lost again the next day. The destruction of the land through war is shown to be so terrible that the survival of any part of nature is almost miraculous. When Jim revisits a field where once peasants had grown their crops he finds 'the area behind the lines ... utterly blasted. The earth was one vast rag and bone shop, the scattered remains of both sides lay all over it'. The shattered forest is equally desolate: 'All the leaves had been blasted from the trees and they stood bare, their trunks snapped like matchwood, their branches jagged, split, or broken off raw and hanging' (pp.109–10). This stands in stark contrast to the beauty and peace of the marshlands in Australia.

Land is important in Australia for other reasons, too. For the original inhabitants of Australia, land is the key to one's sense of self. Respect for the land governs Aboriginal identity and is central to spirituality. Malouf suggests, through Ashley, some sense of this understanding of the significance of land, and through Jim's reverential attitude to the birdlife he expresses the idea that the land has value simply in itself. What is he saying here about the young, English-educated Ashley with his European lifestyle? Perhaps that he symbolises the opportunity the white community has to share with Australia's Indigenous people the richness, security and meaning which the land can provide if they can open their hearts and minds to it and move beyond its value as a financial asset or measure of power.

The traditional rhyme

The traditional rhyme *'Fly away Peter. Fly away Paul. / Come back, Peter. Come back, Paul'* that gives the novel its title has significance on many levels. The association with the birds is the most obvious. They come and go, there is a pattern to their journeys, they travel in pairs. The second last line also symbolises Jim's death. He flies away but does not return. However, the mind is naturally drawn to the last line. There is symmetry in the rhyme, the two-sidedness that is seen in everything. There is balance as Peter and Paul come back. So also in the novel there is loss but the loss is not an empty one. Jim dies, but for Imogen he lives on, because his impact on her life is enduring and transformative.

QUESTIONS & ANSWERS

Essay topics

1 "If he didn't go, he had decided he would never understand, when it was over, why his life and everything he had known were so changed." What does Jim come to understand?

2 'Despite the sadness, the horror and the loss, *Fly Away Peter* is uplifting and optimistic.' Do you agree?

3 'Personal growth can only occur as a result of crisis.' To what extent is this true of Jim Saddler?

4 'Malouf's depiction of war shows that nothing can ever be gained from it.' Do you accept this assessment of the novel?

5 Jim's journey is in many ways an allegory of the emergence of Australia's identity as an independent nation. Explain how both Jim and Australia are changed by their involvement in the war.

6 "*This is what life meant, a unique presence, and it was essential in every creature.*" How is this assessment of the individual married with the passing nature of one life among millions in *Fly Away Peter*?

7 'The interesting part of *Fly Away Peter* is the depiction of war. The novel moves too slowly until we get to that part.' Do you agree?

8 "The war or something like it with a different name would go on growing out from here till the whole earth was involved ... they had fallen, he and his contemporaries, into a dark pocket of time from which there was no escape." What does the war do to Jim?

9 "Enemies, like friends, told you who you were." To what extent is Jim's understanding of self enhanced by his contact with those around him?

10 Evaluate the roles of Ashley and Imogen in the novel. How do they influence Jim's development?

Analysing a sample topic

"Enemies, like friends, told you who you were." To what extent is Jim's understanding of self enhanced by his contact with those around him?

This topic asks you to focus specifically on the relationships Jim Saddler forms throughout the book – the good and the bad, friendly and antagonistic – and explore his growth to self-knowledge as a result of this contact.

To begin with, and very importantly, examine the relationships with Ashley and Imogen. Analyse the bond they share through their work with the birds, their collective vision and what this means for Jim. It allows him to step away from the 'flat' life his father forecasts for him, and to embrace his true talents with confidence. In contrast then, examine the friendships Jim forms when he goes to war and make comparisons. Are they as significant? You must consider Clancy in detail here but you could also look at Eric and Bobby. Do any of these characters emerge as individuals in the same way that Ashley and Imogen do? What is it about Clancy that gives his brief presence in Jim's life such profound impact?

Although the quote refers to 'enemies', Jim in fact only has one personal enemy – Wizzer. The two encounters with him force Jim to confront elements in his character that presumably would otherwise have lain dormant. Examine carefully how this happens and what it means for Jim. What are the respective merits of friendship and hostility in terms of increasing self-awareness? Friends and enemies might both teach us about ourselves but do we learn the same sort of things?

The quotation suggests that Jim learns a great deal about himself through his contact with others. How much of this is raw experience and how much does it reflect the essential character of Jim himself? In order to learn from others we must be receptive, responsive, open to what others might tell us – both good and bad. The relationships with both Ashley and Imogen are examples of how open to others Jim is, despite being 'impenetrably private'. Is it this that so affronts Wizzer and precipitates his first attack?

Another key factor that must be considered is the experience of the war. War is the forum through which Jim confronts the common enemy. It is impossible to isolate the horror and suffering of the trenches from the men who made it so – or conversely made it more bearable.

Jim does develop a clearly defined sense of self and this must be acknowledged. You must trace his personal development from its beginning, largely as a result of his relationships with Ashley and Imogen through to the culmination of his encounters with his fellow soldiers. These consolidate his own awareness and perception of self, and motivate him to consider questions previously outside the range of his understanding or experience.

Finally, make the assessment the question demands: *to what extent* is Jim's self-knowledge enhanced by those around him? Would he have come to a point where he could recognise his essential position in time and place through the discovery of the mammoth fossil had he lived out his life in the innocent tranquillity of the sanctuary? Could he have ever accepted fully the 'limiting nature of things' (p.106) had he not approached the precipice of despair and not been pulled back by the vision of the old man digging and the memory of Imogen Harcourt? Certainly not.

REFERENCES & READING

The text

Malouf, David. *Fly Away Peter*, Penguin Books, Australia, 1983.

Films

Gallipoli, director – Peter Weir; screenplay – David Williamson; starring Mel Gibson and Mark Lee as two innocent young men who go off to war. It depicts the landing at Gallipoli and the wholesale slaughter that occurred.

The Lighthorsemen, director – Simon Wincer; screenplay – Ian Jones; starring Jon Blake, Peter Phelps, Gary Sweet and Sigrid Thornton; tells the story of the attack on Beersheba in Palestine by the Australian Light Horse during World War I.

Both these films will contribute to an understanding of the Australian involvement in World War I, the absurdity of it, the qualities of Australian soldiers which made them famous and which became identified with the Australian personality.

King and Country, director – Joseph Losey; screenplay – Evan Jones; starring Tom Courtney and Dirk Bogart. Made in the 1960s, this black-and-white film remains one of the most powerful statements about trench warfare in the 1914–18 war.

Paths of Glory, director – Stanley Kubrick; screenplay – Stanley Kubrick; starring Kirk Douglas as a Colonel who stands up to a sadistic General in the French Army. The battle scenes are extremely realistic for their time.

Other

1914, Australian Ballet production.

This ballet was performed for the first time in 1998. Based on Malouf's novel, it tells the story in dance of Jim, Ashley and Imogen.